THE FIRST GOLDEN AGE OF BRITISH ADVERTISING

Ruth Artmonsky

'In addition to educating public taste, advertising agents and advertisers have greatly raised the standards of living artists and writers.
The artist no longer needs a patron.
In his modern capacity he is a partner.'

-Sir William Crawford, 1928

Published by Artmonsky Arts
Flat 1, 27 Henrietta Street
London WC2E 8NA
Telephone: 020 7240 8774
Email: artmonskyruth@gmail.com

ISBN 978-0-9935878-6-3

The cover design for this book is based on an illustration
respectfully adapted from Ashley Havinden's *Chrysler 65*
advertisment, 1928. End Papers for the book are based on a
small part of James Fitton's illustration, *A bolt to the blue*.

The illustration opposite is from a set of poster stamps designed
by James Fitton for E & G Berry Ltd, 1928.

My thanks to Margaret Timmers for giving me the idea for
the title and the motivation to put the book together; and to
Brian Webb and Flora Anderson for their enthusiasm and
creativeness in designing it.

Designed by Webb & Webb Design Limited.
Printed in the United Kingdom.

CONTENTS

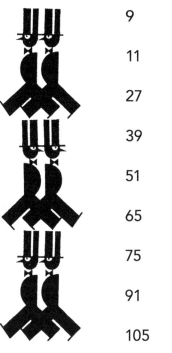

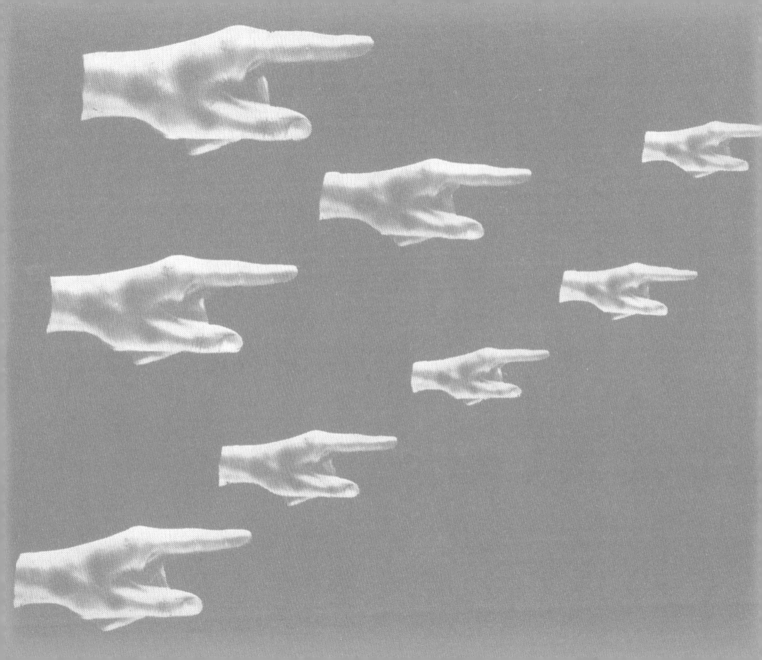

INTRODUCTION

In the introduction to his autobiography, Alan Brooking, [the photographer who 'shot' the pregnant man], writes of the golden age of British advertising, which he dates as starting from the 1950s –

> 'The decade when everything came good, when the kids took over the boardroom, protocol evaporated, brilliant creativity ruled.'

Brooking possibly felt like that because it was the time of the start of his own 'golden age'; and so it goes for all children, whenever and wherever, breaking away from their parents, beginning to find and exert their own individuality, to test out their talents, and to flex their muscles – each generation in turn seems to be intent on creating its own 'new millennium'.

And so it has been in the history of advertising 'families'. Typifying the generation revolts is the family tree stemming from William Crawford – three of his 'children', Colman, Prentis and Varley considered they could do better, and CPV, aided by its brilliant art director, Arpad Elfer, proved they could. But, inevitably they, in turn, were to be challenged by their own children, Collett, Dickenson and Pearce, [CDP], who were to make even more of a stir, along with their art director, Colin Millward. And when CDP was riding high they found they had spawned the young Charles Saatchi, who with his brother Maurice and other CDP 'offspring', were to take over advertising land. The saga of who begat who begat who in advertising was to reach biblical proportions!

So, on reflection, Alan Brooking should not be surprised to hear that others, before him, had considered their time 'golden'; some thirty or forty years before, just prior to, and after, the first World War, other young sparks were in their prime. I have already written about one such, Sir William Crawford, and had planned to follow this with a series of volumes on other advertising entrepreneurs of the inter-war years, but have been waylaid by competing topics of interest. Now, well into my 80s, such a series has become totally impractical, so I have decided to collect together, in one volume, mere sketches of some of the major players of that time, hoping that these brief accounts may stir my own 'next generation' to flesh out and restore the reputation of these entrepreneurs of the 'first golden age of British advertising'.

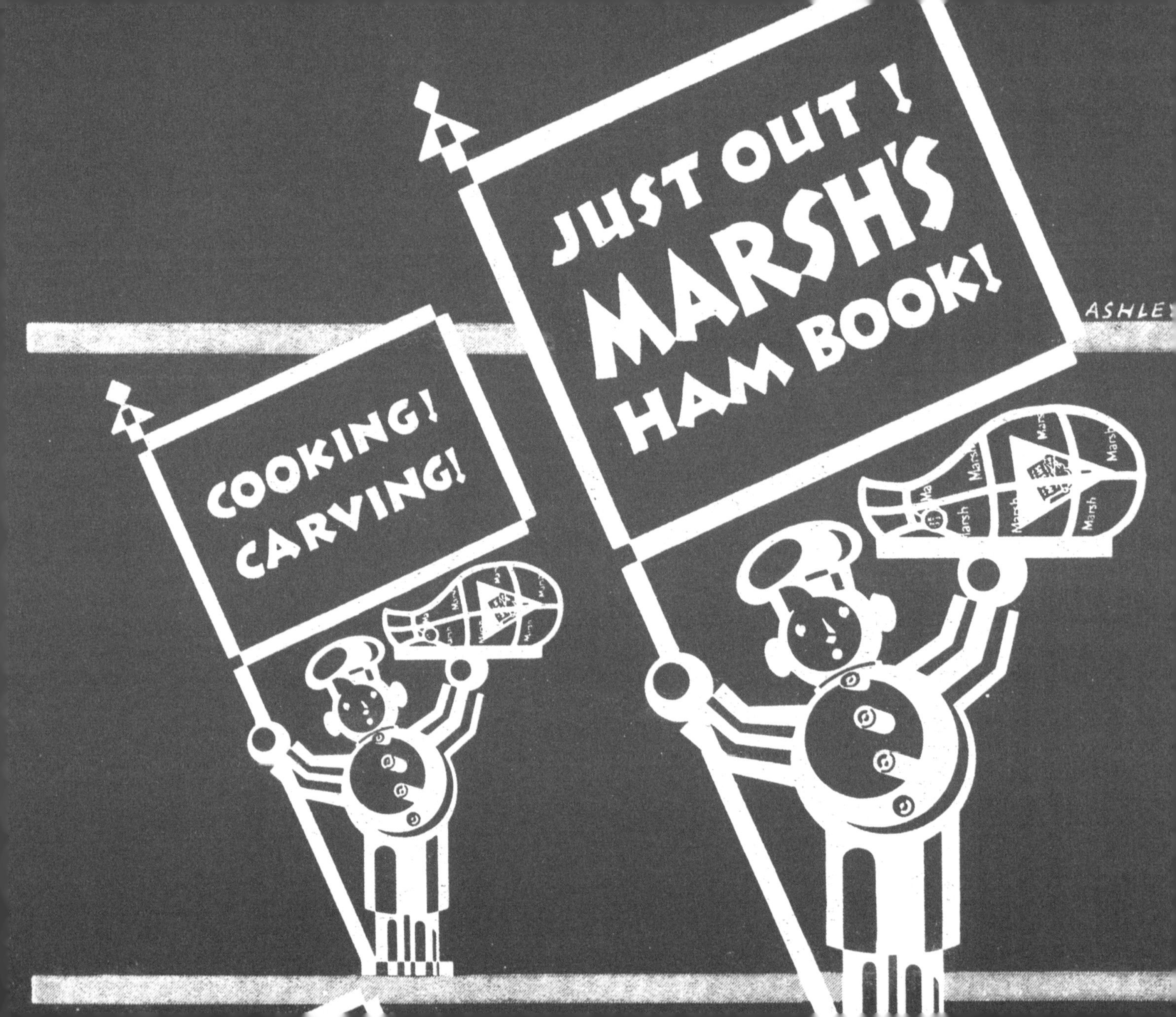
COOKING!
CARVING!
JUST OUT!
MARSH'S
HAM BOOK!
ASHLEY

W. S. CRAWFORD LTD.

William Crawford, born in Glasgow in 1878, as a youth, was not much given to academic study, preferring the action of the sports field. Educated firstly in Scotland and then in Germany, he appears to have left school without any formal qualifications or any specific career in mind. He only entered advertising in his late twenties when he decided to come down to London. He worked in a couple of agencies, first as a space canvasser and then actually carrying accounts, before he set up his own agency in Kingsway in 1914, not the most auspicious starting date.

It was not until World War I ended that Crawford was able to build up his team, his star players, many of whom were to remain loyal to him throughout his life. He tended to prefer untried youth [whose potential he encouraged], women [with an eye on women being major consumers], and people likely to develop specialist skills [which was unusual in advertising at the time].

Crawford's key women were Isabelle Reid [a behind the scenes secretary to his Board and herself to become a Director]; and the two Sangster sisters from Scotland – Florence, [who was

Left: Ashley Havinden for Marsh's Ham, *Punch*, 1928.
Right: Sir William Crawford by 'bil', *Celebrities of Advertising*, 1928

11

'Feeling the pulse' of the foreign customer

Seldom a month goes by but you will find on the deck of some cross-channel steamer a Crawford representative. *He is setting forth* in search of fresh ideas, new outlets, which *will serve and help Crawford's clients.* Advertising to the foreign customer is an intricate art. It must appeal to men and women whose buying habits, whose social and economic values, whose whole manner of life differs profoundly from those of the average Briton. To gauge these differences, to base on them a sound selling scheme, *you have to study the foreigner in his home.* There, where he spends his life, the trained and sensitive advertising man can best observe him—what he eats and drinks, how he dresses, what he earns and how he spends it. Thus, and thus only, can foreign advertising be soundly planned and prepared. Thus, and thus only, can the great overseas markets be made to accept and to demand your goods.

Whoever desires to sell and advertise abroad should consult Crawfords, whose Overseas Department is well-qualified to give you first-class service.

W. S. Crawford Ltd

W S CRAWFORD LTD *Advertising* 233 HIGH HOLBORN LONDON WC1

W.S.Crawford Ltd, 233 High Holborn London WC1 England   Offices and Associates throughout the World

AD.137

Self advertisement for Punch, 1926   Self advertisement by Ashley Havinden, 1953

to become Financial Director and Vice-Chairman of the agency], and Margaret [who moved from accounts executive to Director, specialising in the fashion industry].

Crawford's key young men were Hubert Oughton [to eventually succeed Crawford as Managing Director and Chairman], Saxon Mills [Copy Director] and Ashley Havinden [who was to blossom from a callow untrained youth into one of the most distinguished Art Directors of the 20th century]. Crawford soon got his team in place and created an atmosphere in which they felt able to develop their specific talents. He did not want to have 'yes' men and women, passively responding to clients demands, but personalities who could exert influence, and influence they did!

With a rapidly expanding business Crawford needed larger premises, moving to High Holborn, a building which, by 1930, had been given a striking 'modernist' façade by the architect Frederick Etchells. Equally striking were Crawford's offices in Paris and Germany, he sending the message out, that exciting new buildings implied exciting new ideas from those who worked in them.

From fairly early on Crawford seems to have had international ambitions. Everything he did, wrote about or spoke about was larger than life, his internationalism was ambitious –

'That old communities may be richened; that new communities may leap to life; that the deserts of the world may be gardens – this is our work. Trade is the mainspring of progress.

Advertising is the herald of trade. The pens in our hands are the makers of a new earth.'

By 1921 Crawford had set up an export division aided by his agency's work for Chrysler who were expanding into Europe. Crawford felt no need to adapt his advertising style to different cultures considering its striking simplicity could serve as an international language. Advertising his agency at the start of World War II, he was able to demonstrate, with a map of the world, how extensive his empire had become.

Although Crawford gave a nod to 'intelligence' in advertising, setting up a nominal market research department, his personal style of operating was to rely on intuition. Saxon Mills wrote of Crawford's approach –

'The sudden flash of the shrewd idea; the inspiration gathered from a minute's thought and translated on to the scale of big business.'

What was all-important to Crawford was 'the idea' –

'The advertising idea is the element which secures for your advertising popularity. It puts a desirable, personable, memorable face on your product in the eye of the public. Through it your product wins friends and influences people. It is what personality is to a star or speaker.'

But Crawford wanted more than 'ideas' from his team; they were to be agents of change – their brief from a client may have been to present a finished advertisement within a budget, and to a time limit, but the ambition of the agency was to take their work with their clients well beyond the limits of the initial brief - to a firm's whole marketing strategy and sometimes even to its product range. Margaret Sangster, [Havinden as she became on her marriage to Ashley], is a particularly good example of a Crawford player who managed to reposition a whole industry [fashion] with her ability to see beyond a brief.

Crawford, himself, had ambitions not only for his agency but for the advertising industry as a whole, that it could and should serve as a vehicle for changing society for the better. For Crawford, having a role in Government activities served not only to raise the profile of his agency but of his industry. *Commercial Art* reported in 1925 –

'It marked a new era in British advertising, when Mr. W. S. Crawford was invited by the Government to serve on the Imperial Economic Committee, which Committee will guide and advise the Treasury, through the Prime Minister, in the spending of a £1,000,000 to develop the sale of Empire grown foodstuffs in the United Kingdom.'

Crawford was to become Vice-Chairman of the Empire Marketing Board's Publicity Committee, working alongside

BUT MOTORING MUST GO ON!

War cuts a rift across the lives of all of us. Habits change—almost overnight. New conditions swirl up—settle down upon us.

But *motoring* must go on. The Government wishes that. The nation's business demands it.

So Ford—ever marching on—brings to you the new wartime car—the "Anglia," the latest triumph of Ford engineering.

It is built to give exceptional mileage on 'pool' petrol. It has the all-round economy and modest tax of an efficient 8 h.p. car. It meets the needs of everybody these days.

Yet—see what brilliant Ford engineering has combined with these ! Impressive appear-

ance. Lively performance. Spacious interior. The large outside luggage compartment and generous equipment.

· · ·

A car produced for wartime—and a car which would make its mark in the easy days of peace ! . . .

From the great Ford factory at Dagenham by the Thames large numbers of the "Anglia" are now streaming forth. The Ford dealer in your neighbourhood has one to show you.

See it. Try the "Anglia" ! You *need* this new car for the new times. Britain asks for such a car.

SO...FORD MARCHES ON...

Above: Press advertisement illustrated by H.E Colett for Ford, 1940
Right: Striking press advertisement by Ashley Havinden for Chrysler, 1928

WE ARE COMING
IN THE CHRYSLER!

Frank Pick, its Chairman. Looking back on this period Crawford wrote in a survey *The People's Food*, published in 1938 –

> '... *the period I was privileged to serve on the Imperial Economic Committee and the Empire Marketing Board brought me into contact with new and far-reaching problems of Empire, of trade, of national health, as well as with statesmen, business men, and scientists concerned.*'

Crawford was at the centre of the Empire Marketing Board's multimedia campaigns to get the British buying Empire goods. He and Pick, taught the government, inexperienced in matters of publicity and advertising, how to harness the talents of artists and copy-writers to serve the purpose of government. Crawford's agency no doubt benefitted from all this activity and he, himself, received a knighthood.

This involvement may well have helped towards Crawford landing a government commission in 1933, to publicise the work of the newly established Milk Marketing Board. So energetic was Crawford in carrying out this brief, with the brilliant typography and artwork of Havinden, that *Commercial Art* was prompted to complain –

> '*The morning pint of milk was marked on the capsule, instead of the usual 'Monday delivery', with 'This is milk week'. I did not need to be*

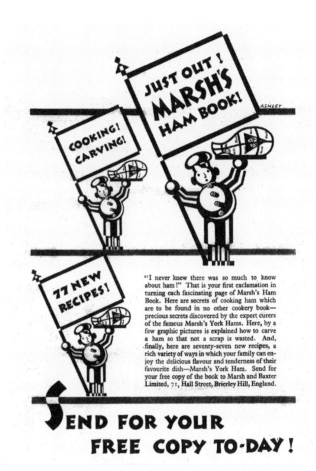

Ashley Havinden for Marsh's Ham, *Punch*, 1928

Ashley Havinden for Enos Fruit Salt, *Punch*, 1926

Ashley Havinden for Enos Fruit Salt, *Punch*, 1927

told for already this was made known to me
by vans noisily hooting, decorated with
milk bottles and streamers, as well as by
posters and newspaper announcements.'

The Post Office was a further government agency with which Crawford's became involved, when its Publicity Relations Department was being developed under the maverick Stephen Tallents. And during World War II Crawford not only worked with other agencies on government campaigns [an arrangement John Gloag referred to as 'a six-cylinder creative energy'], but single handedly ran a number of campaigns for the Ministry of Information, as one publicising the Empire's contribution to the war effort.

Whilst Crawford was active on this wider platform, Ashley Havinden, and a stream of other talented artists, were getting the agency's name abroad for the 'modernism' of its visuals. Many major commercial artists, at one time or another, did work for Crawford's in the inter-war years. Hans Schleger, McKnight Kauffer and H. K. Henrion, along with the distinguished French artists, Jean Carlu and Cassandre, were all called upon during these years.

Schleger and Terence Prentis worked in Crawford's German office, Prentis and his wife Betty, continuing to supply artwork for the agency in London before breaking away to set up their own agency. And it was Crawford who helped create the atmosphere for such a creative outpouring by his championing his specialists –

'In addition to educating public taste advertising
agents and advertisers have greatly raised
the standards of living artists and writers.
The artist no longer needs a patron. In his
modern capacity he is a partner.'*

And further –

'The artist in advertising who puts his pride and
principles and prejudice before this problem [the
client's brief], is putting he cart before the horse...one
day, if he keeps to the problem, he [the artist] will
find, quite suddenly, maybe...that he, in advertising,
is consigning art higher than the artist outside
advertising.'

Crawford had been particularly interested in the typography of his advertisements from the start and his agency was to design, and get constructed its own customised alphabets – Ashley-Crawford and Ashley-Crawford Plain. Morison, the typography guru wrote, in 1952 –

'Things were done to type arrangements,
particularly by the Crawford camp, which
had certainly never been dreamt of before.'

And Crawford was equally supportive of his copywriters.

Initially Crawford wrote his own copy, using the widest possible pen nib, 'wielding it as a weapon rather than merely writing with it'. He was to value 'word power' as much as 'design', encouraging his staff to extend their vocabulary by reading the bible! Saxon Mills name became as synonymous with W. S. Crawford's as Ashley's was with design. Saxon Mills was as grandiose in his pleas for copywriter's status as his boss was for the status of the industry, demanding it produced a Stravinsky or a Corbusier to shake things up; a typical example of his somewhat grandiose ambition was –

'To be a copywriter you need to be able to write. But emphatically it does not follow that because you can write you possess that particular flair for breathing into ten or fifty or a hundred words the power to move a nation…'

Generally the agency went for brevity when it came to copy – 'Stick to Beer', 'Drink Milk Daily' and just 'BASS'. A major exception was its work for Barratt's shoes, where some of the copy ran into hundreds of words. Discussions between various typical members of the public with Mr. Barratt on the problems of walking comfortably, with Mr. Barratt explaining wisely and patiently the health-giving qualities of his reasonably priced yet first class products, were to become familiar advertising features for many decades.

Crawford had clients across the industries but could

Stick to Beer, Ashley Havinden for the Brewers Society, 1939

perhaps be described as having a leaning towards 'fashion' – including, in addition to Barratt's shoes, Kayser stockings, and the stores Liberty's, Jaeger and Simpsons. Crawford's undertook the publicity when Jaeger decided to go 'modern', with new store interiors, window displays and clothes design. *Commercial Art* recorded –

> *'[everything] had the same dynamic dashing*
> *air of being up-to-the-minute, a quality of*
> *gay improvisation.'*

Crawford's appear to have used a number of different artists for its Jaeger campaigns, many now totally forgotten women including Peggy Morris, Phyllis Richards and Eileen Upton. But the Jaeger account began to be 'owned' by the Prentices, and they were to take it with them when they left.

Generally Crawford preferred to work on campaigns rather than one off advertisement assignments, and this was certainly so with the agency's work for Simpson's of Piccadilly. It was Crawford who, in a midnight call with the young Alec Simpson confirmed that the latest product line should be named 'DAKS'; and it was Crawford's that designed the display stand that launched the products, as well as the publicity for the company's strikingly modern new shop; it was said that some one hundred press advertisements appeared in the store's first year. Of course, the dapper Ashley, noted for his passion for clothes, was to the fore in all this, with such other notables as Moholy-Nagy, Felicks

Ashley Havinden for Kayser & Co, 1930

JAEGER'S DESIGNER

SCINTILLATES IN A ROMANTIC MOOD

Jaeger's designer has added the most circean glamours to the human silhouette. She takes a Winterhalter waist and a guardsman's shoulders, a bishop's sleeves and a huntsman's hat and blends them with the luminous inconsequence of utter genius. Lines that swoop and swerve. Capes that flutter with endearingly artificial helplessness. Basques that flute and flare. All the swooning seductions of the eighties with the irrepressible verve of 1931. You don't know how romantic the most modern clothes can be till you've seen the spell-binding collection on the Jaeger Fashion Floor

VISIT THE JAEGER FASHION FLOOR, 352-54 OXFORD STREET, LONDON, W.1
IF YOU LIVE IN SCOTLAND VISIT THE FASHION FLOOR AT 119, PRINCES ST , EDINBURGH

Reading from left to right: LE WINNER, MAYFLOWER, TRÈS SPORT, MATINALE, LA VIE PARISIENNE

VISIT THE JAEGER FASHION FLOOR, 352-54 OXFORD STREET, LONDON, W.1
IF YOU LIVE IN SCOTLAND VISIT THE FASHION FLOOR AT 119, PRINCES ST , EDINBURGH

Press advertisement by Eileen Upton for Jaeger, 1933

Betty Prentis for Jaeger, 1932

Terence Prentis for H. J. Nicoll & Co Ltd, 1932

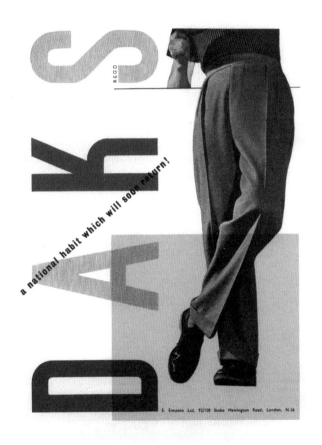

Ashley Havinden for DAKS, 1947

We don't know where the High Hats get their high hats—but we do know where they get their cigars . . . Have not Larrañagas been shipped from Havana since 1834 to the continual delight of the Haute Noblesse?

LARRAÑAGA

HAVANA CIGARS

In Larrañaga you have the flavour of the true Havana leaf at its finest. Rolled on its native soil, as it always has been — for Larrañaga is the oldest established brand in Havana today. Yet these superb cigars are as accessible to the man of moderate means as to the millionaire. They are made in all shapes and sizes and at all prices — in boxes of 25, 50, 100—each box bearing the green guarantee stamp of the Government of Cuba—without which no Havana cigar is authentic. You couldn't find more magnificent gifts for Christmas than Larrañaga Cigars.

Ashley Havinden for Havana Cigars, *Punch*, 1932

'untin'-fishin'-shootin'

Press advertisement by Ashley Havinden for Simpsons, 1937

Topolski, Frank Ford [the cartoonist], and Hof, who was to become Simpson's main illustrator for around a quarter of a century.

Crawford died in 1950 and in its tribute to him the *Advertisers Weekly* declared –

> '*Sir William did more than any other man of this*
> *century to raise the quality of British advertising*
> *and to enhance its prestige throughout the world.*'

Crawford not only lifted the status of advertising, but helped make it an agent of change. Over time Crawford was here, there and everywhere; there was not a club, society or professional body in any way connected to advertising of which he was not a member, frequently holding office. So nationally important did he consider his industry that, at times, he could be said to have confused his own role with that of a politician.

He was a near impossible act to follow, but Hubert Oughton, who had worked closely with him since the 1920s and was his successor, made a sterling attempt through to 1968, by which time Crawford's had merged financially with Dorland Advertising with which it had been associated for many years. The History of Advertising Trust, which holds relevant material, has it that the agency was still in operation under the name W. S. Crawford through to the 1980s.

Right: Self advertisement in *Graphics RCA Fifteen years of work of the School of Graphic Design, Royal College of Art*, designed by John Hutchinson, 1963

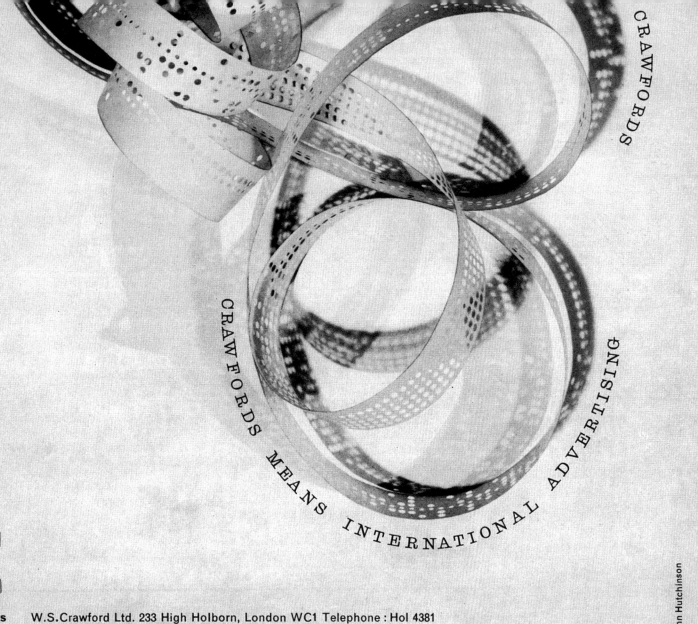

CRAWFORDS

CRAWFORDS MEANS INTERNATIONAL ADVERTISING

John Hutchinson

Crawfords   W.S.Crawford Ltd. 233 High Holborn, London WC1 Telephone : Hol 4381
Offices and Associates throughout the World

FOR ALL THE FUN & ALL THE THRILLS

THE CIRCUS BY BERTRAM W. MILLS

NOW OPEN

DSCHANG SCHENG-HAI YUNG CHINESE HAIR RAISERS

THE CHAVALLI TROUPE   THE ANDREU TRIO

CON COLLEANO

WALKER'S BEARS

THE DAKOTAS

THE PYKETTI TROUPE

CATALINI

HOLTERSTEIN

THE ROMEOS

TOGARE

THE FRANK JACKSON TROUPE

CARMO'S HORSES

CHARLIE RIVELS

2.30 7.30 OLYMPIA

There isn't a show anywhere so breathlessly exciting
the Circus that put the 'O' in Olympia. You've seen
the old circus stunts! Olympia will show you thrills a
fun you've never had before!

See what Bertram W. Mills has gathered from the en
of the Earth to stagger and amuse London. See new an
unheard of turns, new feats that bring the intrepi
performers to what seems for a thrilling moment t
very brink of catastrophe.

And then, laugh it all off—split your sides in fact at th
Mirthquake of Merriment contrived by the most comic
clownish, and jolly fellows in the world. Twenty-
wonder turns—the high water mark of Circus Sensatio
and Arenic Amusement.

Reserved Seats 10/6, 7/6, 5/9, 3/6. Unreserved
BOX OFFICE TELEPHONE : RIVERSIDE 2729, and l
leading agencies and libraries. Book right now!

GREENLY'S LTD.

Although Arthur Greenly, unlike Crawford, was not much of a self-publicist, others thought highly of him. A retrospective article on his agency in *Art & Industry* in 1953 described him as –

'*...a man of considerable force of character and ability and who is considered one of the pioneers of modern advertising in this country.*'

A. J. Greenly set up his agency in 1914 [occasionally it is dated 1909], in the Strand, moving it to Chancery Lane in 1928, and, in the post-war years, to an impressive six-storey building in Berkeley Street, Mayfair [c1952].

From the start Greenly was determined that his Directors should each carry their own group of clients, should be hands-on, and this structure was maintained through to the 1950s. It was

considered that Directors were likely to have widely different temperaments and interests and that the Board as a whole should allot each new account to the one they considered best suited to handle it. Greenly seems to have been something of a pseudo-psychologist in this, and his concern for the individuality of his Directors was extended to his clients needs. His off-repeated maxim was –

'*Individuality is to advertising what personality is to a man.*'

He considered it key to successful advertising that an agency had as full an understanding of its clients and their customers as possible, yet another maxim being 'the head sends the message which opens the purse'. Greenly was to put some of these considerations into his book *Psychology as a Sales Factor*, first published in 1927. His evangelism for 'individuality' for clients and campaigns became imbued through his agency. 1934 finds one of his staff, R. A. Allen, spreading the notion –

Left: Bertram W. Mills Circus, press advertisement, 1929
Above: A. J. Greenly, *Display*, October 1931- July 1932

Conference Room on the sixth floor of Greenly's new office,
Berkeley Street, 1953

Reception on the sixth floor of Greenly's new office,
Berkeley Street, 1953

'...people are interested in a product or service only
in so far as it affects their appearances, their comfort,
their pleasure ...Every successful advertisement
ever written talks intelligently to one individual.'

'New and original thoughts are not required – in fact
they are often lost to the mass mind – advertising only
requires average thoughts expressed in the best possible
way – and there is room for ingenuity in that alone.'

Although Greenly stressed the importance of advertising
personnel gaining some understanding human nature, his
argument docs not seem to have resulted in any particular
extra subtlety or sophistication in the agency's productions.
When asked to reflect on the whole business of advertising by
Commercial Art in 1931, he wrote –

Greenly doesn't seem to have had the grandiose ambitions
for advertising held by other agency entrepreneurs, but
nevertheless he still saw it as more than just aiding the sale of
goods and services but further as a means of keeping the masses

Right: An exhibition design staging the Past Present and Future
of Publicity, held at the Royal Society of Watercolour Painters, 1930

TOWARDS 2030 A.D.

GREENLYS

National Advertising, Greenly's self
advertisement, 1928

Face to Face, Self advertisement for the
Evening Standard, 1930

informed, of educating people as to what were the advances in science and technology, and so on; and through its contribution to expanding markets and increasing sales resulting in price reduction, he saw advertising as essential for raising the general standard of living.

If Greenly was not a particularly high profile personality himself, he, nevertheless, saw it that his agency was continually in the public eye. Greenly's was to advertise its activities in the national press, less frequently used by other agencies for self-promotion. A typical Greenly's campaign was one appearing regularly in the *Evening Standard* with the tag 'Watch Greenly's work for clients', with the top half image and the bottom copy. This met with some approval, especially as to the typography used –

> *'The whole is assembled with what is the essence of good typography – clarity, balance and the employment of no contorted stridencies in the type used, not a grain more emphasis than necessary...There is no talking 'at' one. The tone of the wording somehow ranges the reader and the advertiser on a common plane.'*

Another medium for Greenly's self-publicity was exhibitions. Occasionally it would hire the gallery of the Royal Society of Watercolour Painters in Pall Mall to show off its work for clients. In 1930, one such show was more ambitious, providing for visitors a comprehensive history of advertising.

See Greenly's *about* Advertising, Self advertisement, 1950

Commercial Art showed a qualified approval –

> *'...in the place of the chaste and tame little*
> *water-colours that one was accustomed to see*
> *in Pall Mall one came with a pleasant shock*
> *of surprise to press advertisements with the*
> *most aggressively fertile and modern ideas.'*

And –

> *'Some of the advertisements were a little too*
> *exuberant in imagination and had become*
> *so overcrowded that the effect was lost.'*

By using the watercolourists' gallery, Greenly, virtually promoting advertising art as 'fine' art, produced catalogues for the exhibitions one actually spelling this out –

> *'...the old lasting principles of all beautiful*
> *things – Balance, Simplicity, Restraint.*
> *Out of them all is coming this new art-*
> *form, this true expression of our time.'*

And he seems to have put his money where his mouth was in promoting the status of commercial art. Howard Wadman, who had joined Greenly's as a junior and was to rise to become its Art Director reminisced in 1940 –

> *'In 1928 the late A. J. Greenly sent me to Berlin*
> *to absorb the new gospel. As a young hopeful*
> *of twenty one I found the architecture, the*
> *typography, the posters and the shop windows of*
> *the modern movement extremely interesting.'*

In spite of all of this, Greenly's never produced an artist of the calibre of McKnight Kauffer or Ashley Havinden; nor, although Greenly professed an interest in the use of photography, anyone of the talent of Arpad Elfer of Colman, Prentis & Varley. Yet Greenly appears to have had, at times, the aspiration of a Frank Pick of London Transport or a Jack Beddington of Shell. A Greenly's Director, one F. E. Ball, in 1934, spoke of the agency's scheme to make use of 'famous men' for its art work. It had, with a certain trepidation, approached a number of artists to see who might cooperate and it is interesting, to the current reader, to note who was included in its list who agreed –

Bernard Meninsky

Charles Ginner

Iain McNab

Ethelbert White

Gerald Moira

James Pryde

C. R. W. Nevinson

Anton Lock

Mark Gertler

John Armstrong

Walter Bayes

Clare Leighton

Leonard Squirrel

Press advertisements for Excelsior Shoes 1929, Craven "A" Cigarettes 1931
and Windsmoor 1953

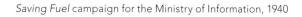

Saving Fuel campaign for the Ministry of Information, 1940

Illustration by T. L. Poulton for George Ellison Ltd, 1936

Magazine advertisement for The General Electric Co, 1953

Illustration by Kevin McDonnough for the A.C.V Group, 1953

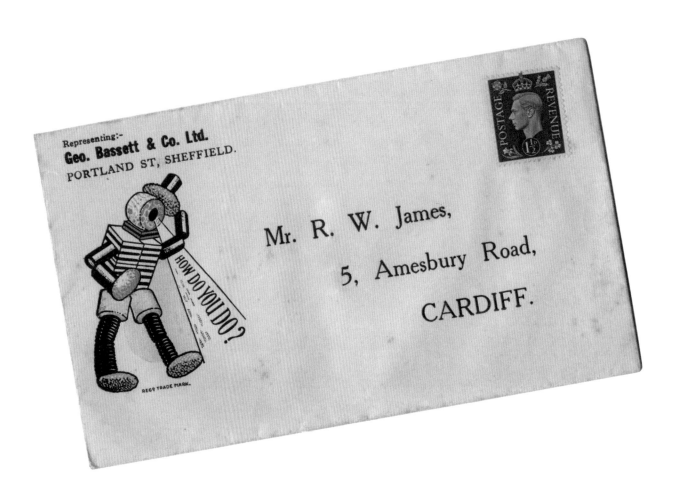

An advertising envelope from Bertie Bassett, 1939

A number of these were wood engravers, which was popular in advertising at the time. Yet, as it turned out, very few of the listed artists did much 'commercial' work at all, let alone for Greenly's.

Apart from its own self-advertising, Greenly's appears to have run few accounts or campaigns that would distinguish it from any other agency. It perhaps did a little more 'display' work than others, deploying the fact that the Europeans were so far ahead in this medium; it did produce some interesting work for Craven A cigarettes, and, during the war, for the Ministry of Information on saving fuel. And it was Greenly's which conceived the 'roof-umbrelled' couple for Abbey National.

However, Greenly's did give us Bertie Bassett. Liquorice Allsorts were first produced by Geo. Bassett & Co. Ltd of Sheffield, the apocryphal account of the birth of the product being that one of its salesmen dropped a tray of samples resulting in the mix. The idea of Bertie is recorded as coming from a copy-writer, Frank Regan, who is said to have constructed the original Bertie from the sweets and a number of pipe-cleaners. Loraine Conran, *Commercial Art's* regular commentator on graphic design, wrote scathingly of Bertie in 1935 –

> '*Bertie Bassett is as bad as his jokes…the Bassett artist has failed altogether to get any vitality or movement into his creation.*'

The rest of the world was to disagree, for Bertie became one of advertising's handful of truly iconic characters. Greenly's, who placed 'continuity' very close to 'individuality', kept faith with Bertie, and by the 1950s *Art & Industry* was taking a rather different view –

> '*The lively figure of Bertie Bassett, first created some eighteen years ago and always shown in action, exemplifies the policy of continuity in advertising.*'

With Greenly dead before the onset of WWII, the agency seems to have survived reasonably well through the 1950s but, by 1962, was engulfed by the Lonsdale-Hands Organisation, which although a relative newcomer [founded by the designer Richard Lonsdale-Hands in 1953] had grown to be one of the leading British commercial design groups. The Greenly's name was still appearing into the 1980s.

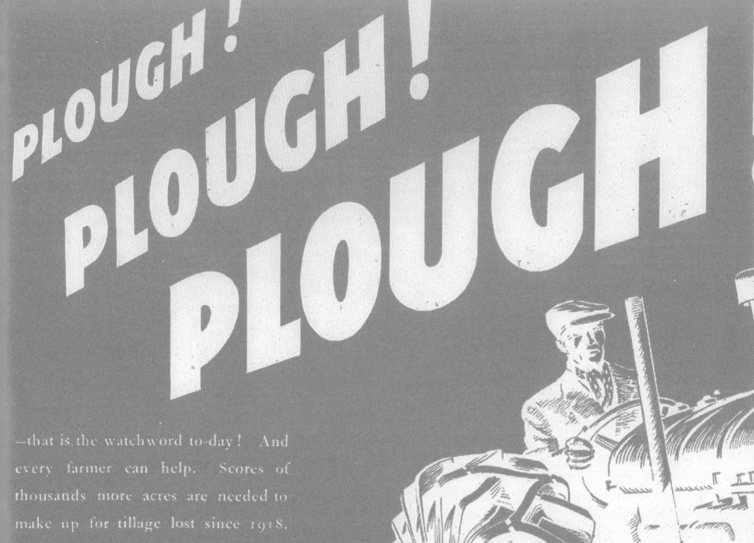

PLOUGH!
PLOUGH!
PLOUGH!

—that is the watchword to-day! And every farmer can help. Scores of thousands more acres are needed to make up for tillage lost since 1918. We simply MUST produce more food and fodder at home to free our money and shipping for vital arms.

CHARLES F. HIGHAM

*'A man of energy. A man of audacity…
a vast electric sign amidst the twinkling
lights of publicity. A force that would
change the axis of the earth as a 'stunt'
and stop the sun in its course in order
to draw attention'*

Commercial Art 1928

*'For nearly thirty years the destiny and the
activities of the Higham agency were
dominated by one giant personality. Few
who knew him would deny that Sir Charles
Higham bestrode like a Colossus, not only
the organization he founded in 1909, but
also the advertising world as a whole.'*

Art & Industry 1952

Left: Plough Now campaign, Ministry of Agriculture and Fisheries, 1941
Right: Charles. F. Higham by Aubrey Hammond, 1928

39

Charles Frederick Higham, the man so lauded, came relatively late to advertising. Born in Walthamstow in 1876, his family emigrated to the United States on the death of his father, around 1885. There is no detailed picture of the young Higham's life in America, but it is thought that he left school about thirteen, trying his hand at a number of jobs [in a pharmacy, a hotel and on a newspaper], and even that he served in the U.S. army. One report has it that he had had some twenty nine jobs before he was thirty!

What is known is that he returned to London in 1906 and started selling advertising space [on theatre curtains], and is thought to have had a spell at W.H.Smith's, which, at the time, had its own advertising and studio departments. Before the onset of WWI, he had set up his own agency in Imperial House, Kingsway and was soon bragging that he was running 'the leading service in London', having bagged such clients as Remington Typewriters and Austin Reed.

By 1921 Higham had got himself a knighthood for what had been his contribution to the war effort. Quite apart from his work for government publicity, he had organised the first battalion of volunteers. But it was his work on the Committee for Recruitment Propaganda and as Director of Publicity for the National Savings Committee, particularly with its Victory Loan Committee, that earned him his honour. He was described as –

'...the super advertising man who taught the British government how to harness the immense power of scientific publicity to the chariot of war.'

And Higham's reputation was further enhanced when he became President of the Associated Advertising Clubs of the World in 1924, bringing its convention to London, for publicising the British Empire Exhibition of the same year which kick-started the Advertising Association, and by the considerable personal acclaim he received [much generated by his own account] of his whirlwind visit to the States to boost the sale of tea. He reported that in thirty days he had spoken to some 6000 advertising men, newspaper publishers, merchants and retailers, had made several broadcasts, and written a number of articles, as a result of which 300 teashops grew to 8000!

Higham had had a shot at politics, serving as Conservative M.P. for Islington South from 1918 to 1922, but had stood down presumably to devote himself to his rapidly expanding agency and, indeed, proselytising the importance of advertising generally. Apart from numerous talks and articles Higham wrote four books on his passion, at least one of which might still serve as a textbook for young advertising aspirants today –

1918	Scientific Distribution
1920	Looking Forward:
	Mass Education through Publicity
1929	Advertising and the Man In the Street
1929	Advertising: Its Use and Abuse

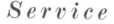
Self advertisement, 1916

Self advertisement ,1952

Higham was promoting advertising as a 'scientific' tool that could have significant influence –

'…advertising is one of the mightiest and consequently one of the most dangerous forces in the modern world.'

He made what he could of the pseudo-psychology of the time suggesting that advertising should use the power of the imagination to reach people's unconscious needs and desires –

'Psychology gives advertising an intellectual basis by revealing the laws that govern mental processes.'

And yet Higham tended to be straightforward his advertising, calling a spade a spade, and the advertisements coming from his agency were generally devoid of 'frills and jazziness', as he referred to much of the then current output. For Higham an advertisement had to be commanding – clear headlines, large typography, sensational captions – directive not apologetic. He considered that people did not want to think, and that lightness and whimsy were inappropriate. As he wrote in *The Post* in 1938 –

'…buying is a very serious operation to every man and woman, wherefore humour in posters [and advertising generally] is all wrong.'

What needed to be communicated should be put over with punch, clarity and economy –

'I claim that Higham advertising fills white space profitably. It creates new markets. It strengthens existing ones without waste inservice, money or words.'

As long as Higham was holding the reins, everything that left his agency was signed off by him, and a Higham advertisement could always be recognized by a small CFH at the bottom right-hand corner – few other agents were so allowed to advertise themselves at their client's expense.

And yet Higham's self-assuredness in how advertising worked best that drove his own agency so successfully was to become formulaic and other agencies, particularly those more interested in the aesthetics of advertising, were to overtake him.

Illustrative of this is when Stuart's replaced Higham's for Imperial Airways publicity. Oliver Green wrote of this –

'Charles Higham provided consultancy services to the company through his agency, but his old-fashioned approach to advertising, which relied on wordy testimonials and purple prose in press advertisements, would have been inappropriate to promoting a new airline. Visual promotion through posters or well-illustrated magazines was not his style.'

Dunlop Tyres, *Punch*, 1930

Dunlop Tyres, *Punch*, 1933

FAMOUS FORTS

RYE CASTLE
Edward I built the Ypres Tower and Land Gate which still remain as a memento of the age when Rye was a fortified port.

Today, just as in the days of Edward I, safety is the prime personal consideration. Hence DUNLOP Tyres. In this age of speed, the modern motorist will get, in DUNLOP Fort Tyres, his best safeguard against the risks of the road. For long service, safety, comfort and economy, fit DUNLOP.

DUNLOP *Fort* TYRES

Famous Forts Campaign featuring Rye Castle, 1937

Where Higham did score was with Dunlops, an account for which his agency is best remembered, and which it carried from the 1920s through to WWII by which time Dunlop was carrying out a good deal of its advertising itself.

John Boyd Dunlop, whose surname was adopted by the company, was a vet in Belfast who had constructed a primitive pneumatic tyre for his child's tricycle and, in fact, had very little to do with the development of the company. Pneumatic Tyre became Booth's Cycle Agency, which, by 1901, had morphed into Dunlop Rubber, run largely by the du Clos dynasty who had bought Dunlop out.

Charles F. Higham Ltd appears to have been first commissioned by Dunlop in the early 1920s. The agency made much of the Britishness of the product which, by then, was in competition with Michelin, Goodyear and Pirelli. A 1923 advertisement appearing in *Punch*, with a clear CFH in the right-hand bottom corner, had a Union Jack draping a tyre with a large heading – 'Does it say MADE IN ENGLAND on your tyres'. The advertisement, curiously and generously, listed, in small type at the bottom, some twenty six other British tyre firms.

And along with the Britishness of the product Higham chose to add such qualities as 'strength' and 'solid reliability' – making much play on the word 'Fort', Fort Dunlop being the extensive manufacturing works of the company. A splendid example is a two-colour magazine advertisement of 1930 showing a tyre as the 'O' in Dunlop in large three-dimensional letters over a pink and grey drawing of the immense Fort Dunlop site. Using colour in tyre advertising was rare, and this the agency continued to do in a series of advertisements in 1933, the pink replaced by a strong red with the patriotic tag – 'Buy British, Buy Dunlop'. And then again Higham was to use the notion of 'fort' in a series of full-page advertisements appearing in 1937 in such nationals as the *Illustrated London News* entitled 'Famous Forts'; for these Higham seems to have allowed a more poetic flowing copy as with one of a watercolour of Rye castle –

> *'Today, just as in the days of Edward I, safety is the prime consideration. In this age of speed, the modern motorist will get, in DUNLOP Fort Tyres, his best safeguard against the risks of the road, For long service, safety, comfort and economy, fit DUNLOP.*

An altogether shorter Higham campaign, but one that had impact, was for the Millers Mutual Association that was launched in the year he died, 1938, yet it was still initialled by him; it carried the tag 'Bread for Energy'. And during the war, the agency was again to be in the news with its 'Plough the Land' campaign for the Ministry of Agriculture and Fisheries, when an appeal was made to farmers to increase their war efforts on the home front. Advertising World wrote of the campaign –

> *'...scientifically directed persuasion can do more than make a legal requirement seem only right and necessary – it can encourage the subject of*

The record breaking Hillman Minx, 1937

the law to exceed what the constitution requires of
him, and to do it willingly with a good heart.'

In his book *Looking Forward, mass education through publicity*, Higham expanded his argument for government publicity through, presumably, the skills of advertising. Astutely dedicating the book to Lloyd George, he pointed out that government had no formal machinery for 'speaking to the people' and needed to realize that public opinion was 'a mighty force, the greatest force, the most powerful influence in the community' and therefore needed to be handled adroitly. Panning the press as a vehicle for such influence Higham reminded his readers that –

'When during the war facts had to be given to
the public with startling and sudden emphasis,
the advertising columns were employed.'

In addition to the advertising columns of the press becoming the state's preferred medium for its publicity, Higham went further, and argued for a State Publicity Bureau [thus foreseeing the Ministry of Information]. He blatantly declared –

'The time will come when Governments will publish
all the news themselves. They will have their own
Publicity Department, staffed by expert advertising
men. All their announcements will appear as
advertisements in special type… Advertisements

honourably used, developed along subtle lines, may
yet prove the chief factor in the Government of the
future…'

With Higham's death in 1938 and the restrictions placed on advertising activity during WWII, the Charles F. Higham agency seems to have lost steam. If there were any changes in the way the agency operated it might be said to have become a shade more 'arty'. It was not that Higham had been unaware of the development of 'art in advertising' taking place in the 1920s and 30s, for in *Advertising, its uses and abuses* he lists most of the major commercial artists of the time; he just seems to have considered words more important, and there is no doubt that is where his skills lay.

Whereas the agency had rarely featured in the graphic design press prior to WWII, in the 1950s examples of its work, particularly for Dunlop and VAT69, were featured fairly regularly in such publications as *Modern Publicity*, the agency using its own 'pool of visualisers' with Norman Wilson as Art Director, as well as artists drawn from the Carlton Studios.

Higham's was eventually absorbed into the Osborne Group and its name disappeared forever when the Group merged it with Osborne-Peacock and Dunn-Meynell Keefe, to form Osborne Advertising in 1972.

Bread for Energy campaign for the Millers Mutual Association, Illustration by Veale Gilchrist, 1940

In the reign of George the Third Bass was served in jugs like this.

With the French Revolution as the chief topic for talk, BASS came to the table in jugs like this. See the hops and barley motif in the fine design.

Your BASS to-day is served perhaps in less interesting jugs and glasses . . . but it *still* has the same stimulating and refreshing qualities which through more than 150 years have changed only for the better. Drink BASS regularly . . . it tones you up, revives your spirit and enables you **to** resist seasonal ailments.

LET YOUR DAILY DRINK BE

In Wellington's time – they enjoyed BASS out of glasses like this.

The collectors call this an 18th century ale-glass "straight-sided, with rectangular bowl." A rare glass now, it often brought BASS to appreciative lips.

TODAY—though the glasses are less grand —BASS remains the same refreshing and invigorating beverage as when first brewed in 1777.

A daily glass of BASS gives you the best of everything that makes good beer.

LET YOUR DAILY DRINK BE

Let Your Daily Drink Be Bass, A series of Press advertisement for the
Bass Brewery, 1936

'...when, on the invitation of the BBC, I gave a broadcast on 'Advertising and Industry' I had the ear of the largest audience ever addressed by an advertising agent in these islands. Debating a subject in which many people in these islands are interested, but few understand, there occurred to me the idea of taking the back page of this supplement [to the Daily Mail] so that its millions of readers may learn more about this thing called Advertising from one who has spent the greater part of his life in it. For egotism of this kind no apology is needed.'

Charles F. Higham
June 14th, 1937

Plough for Victory, A Dunlop contribution to the Ministry of Agriculture and Fisheries Campaign, 1941

THE LONDON PRESS EXCHANGE

'If, as Voltaire suggested, God is on the side of the big battalions it may be worth mentioning that the total staff of the London Press Exchange is some 600 people.'

Art & Industry 1953

T he London Press Exchange [LPE], one of the more modest, least self-congratulatory of advertising agencies was, in fact, by the onset of WWII one of the largest operating in Great Britain. It had been founded by R. J. Sykes and Frederick Higginbottom in one room in the Strand in 1892, and after moves first to Fleet Street and then to Charing Cross, it settled, in 1924, in St.Martin's Lane.

Sykes and Higginbottom were both young journalists who may well have met up through their work for the *Irish Press*. Higginbottom was soon to disappear from the annuls of LPE, developing his career at the *Pall Mall Gazette*, and, from 1919 until his retirement in 1930, at the *Daily Chronicle*.

Little is recorded of Reginald James Sykes, who, after a private school education and a period working in commercial city offices became a reporter for the *Irish National Press* and other papers. And, indeed, it was as a reporter that he founded LPE as a news agency, providing largely sports news for provincial newspapers. And Sykes reporting background was to come to influence his style of operating as an advertising man. *Commercial Art* in 1936, reflecting on Sykes career describing him 'still a reporter' –

> *'…interested in all information that comes his way, and in much that he makes come his way.'*

Sykes was someone who preferred to operate from a solid data base, carefully mulled over. He mistrusted spontaneity and flair, saying of the latter 'heaven knows what it means'.

It is not a surprise then to learn that LPE is considered to have been the birthplace of British market research, and generally rated one of the most research-minded advertising agency. Much of this development was steered by Major George Harrison, who had joined LPE as an assistant secretary in 1920, becoming, by 1923, a member of the Board, and, in 1930,

Left: Mr Richard Lawrence Sykes, Chairman of The London Press Exchange, 1936

Managing Director; on Sykes death in 1940, he combined this role with that of Chairman. In 1951 he was to retire as Managing Director but remain as Chairman.

In 1933 LPE carried out its first large-scale readership survey, published in three-volumes the following year - *A Survey of Reader Interest in the National Morning and London Evening Press*; and in 1936 Harrison co-authored with F. C. Mitchell and the statistical staff at LPE *The Home Market; a handbook of statistics*, the first major study of the British as consumers. Pioneers of large scale agency research, some of LPE's surveys canvassed as many as 25,000 responses to advertisements.

All of this activity was advanced by LPE taking on board a social scientist in 1933, one Mark Abrams. Abrams had studied at the London School of Economics before spending a couple of years [1931-3] at the Brookings Institution, a well-established think-tank in Washington. Abrams, considered the pioneer of market research in Britain, was seconded by LPE to the BBC during WWII but returned in 1946 and set up Research Services Ltd. This seems, at least initially, to have functioned as an independent vehicle within LPE, conducting surveys for its major clients.

In fact LPE operated in its early years via several subsidiaries. By the 1950s these, together, were referred to as the 'LPE Group' and consisted of Outdoor Publishing Ltd [concerned with bill-posting]; Technical and General Advertising Company; St.James Advertising and Publishing Ltd. [focused on financial firms]; Industrial and Educational Film Co. [pioneers of advertising film]; Publicity Arts Ltd and Fanfare Press [offering commercial art and printing services]; Research Services Ltd. [providing market research and press statistics]; and Intam Ltd.[dealing with overseas advertising].

LPE was not considered the most progressive when it came to the 'visuals' of advertising. Publicity Arts had started as completely independent of LPE, run by an ex-Slade School of Art student, H. E. Collett, to provide art and design services, using both its staff artists along with free-lancers. It came to be much used by LPE and by another advertising agency, Paul E. Derrick. As a consequence it moved its offices from the Strand to St.Martin's Lane to better serve the two. In 1923 a Publicity Arts self-advertisement was from 108-110 St. Martin's Lane which was LPE's location. It described its services –

> '... *the careful blending of straightforward business information with artistic planning is one of the chief reasons for our success as producers of sales literature.*'

When Publicity Arts became a part of LPE is not clear, nor the relationship between LPE's own art staff and those of Publicity Arts. Certainly by the mid-1920s the artwork of LPE advertisements was ascribed to LPE rather than to Publicity Arts. It was LPE that was to give us Mr. Therm, initially designed by Eric Fraser in the 1930s, and Phillip Boydell's the Squander Bug in WWII [Boydell variously described as being employed by LPE

Self advertisement, 1928

THE SERVICE
that we offer

THIS, THAT YOU ARE READING, is an unusual advertisement—unusual in that only three people were concerned in its production. Almost all the advertising campaigns we do for our clients involve the work of perhaps ten times that number. For we have the most complete service in Great Britain to offer. What we do here is complemented by the work of our specialist companies, each at the top of its own professional tree, each working also for its own clients.

Thus, **Research Services Limited** supply us with exact statistics about markets and press readership.

Publicity Arts Limited and The Fanfare Press turn rough scribbles for print, packaging and display material into beautifully finished reality.

Outdoor Publicity Limited have put a new exactness into the assessment of poster-site visibility.

Intam Limited, with their world-wide connections, offer an exceptionally well-informed overseas advertising service.

St. James's Advertising & Publishing Company Limited have for years been masters of the intricacies of financial advertising and the reporting of company meetings.

Technical & General Advertising Agency Limited are expert at interpreting technicalities with accuracy and imagination.

And finally we have a close working arrangement with **Film Producers Guild Ltd,** whose educational and technical films have won several Festival Awards.

IT IS UNLIKELY that you will need the services of all these specialists. It is even more unlikely that your advertising would not be the better for the work of some of them.

THE LPE
GROUP OF COMPANIES

The London Press Exchange Ltd
110 ST MARTIN'S LANE · LONDON · WC2 · TEMPLE BAR 2424

Self advertisement, 1952

Mr Therm by his creator, Eric Fraser, 1937

or by the National Savings Committee]. LPE also made use of several of the major commercial artists of the time – McKnight Kauffer, Dora Batty, T. L. Paulton, Horace Taylor and Jean Carlu. Percy Bradshaw, the art-in-advertising guru, wrote, in the 1920s, that many of the best known artists of the time actually did their first advertising work for LPE.

Phillip Boydell actually joined LPE in 1926, becoming its Art Director, and remaining there through to his retirement in 1961. A colleague described him –

'He has more energy and more mental energy, than any man has a right to have.'

A dapper little man with a shock of red hair, Boydell not only bubbled with ideas himself, but was considered a fine motivator of others. Not only is he remembered for the Squander Bug [a character used to encourage people to invest in government savings bonds], but as art director for the Black Widow poster [a road safety poster that told it as it was], and for Festival, the official typeface used at the Festival of Britain.

Altogether less well-documented is LPE's pioneering work with advertising film through the Industrial and Educational Film Co. Ltd. Bradshaw reported that by the mid-1920s LPE had produced films for over fifty clients that had been shown in 'upward of two thousand cinemas'. That Keith Lucas, the first Professor of Film & Television at the Royal College of Art and later Director of the British Film Institute worked for a time at LPE appears incidental, for he is credited as having been employed as a copywriter!

When it comes to clients LPE seems to have been fairly broadly based – some drinks firms [including Barclay's Lager and Findlater's Port]; some early car advertising [for Singer, Lancia, Daimler and Vauxhall]; major confectionary companies [as Rowntree's and Cadbury's]; and some fashion [including Saxone and Lotus shoes and Berlei foundation garments]. And along with 'Mr. Therm' and the 'Squander Bug', National Benzol's 'Mercury' was another character introduced by LPE.

LPE does seem, however, to have had more than its share of the advertising of cigarettes and tobacco. It worked for a number of different brands, several, as Abdulla, de Reske and Greys, came to be absorbed into Godfrey Phillips, others, as Three Nuns, becoming part of the Imperial Group. This last was considered to have had some of the most distinctive brand advertising in the industry. Associating the product with the church was, perhaps, to ascribe it an air of respectability. From about 1927 LPE shifted the focus from 'the church' to 'the thinker' – the man of ideas. Three Nuns was one of the more highly priced brands and it was thought that 'the man of ideas' being a discriminating character would be prepared to pay more for the 'tranquility' smoking the brand would bring. A number of artists were used, including, earlier on, Alfred Thomson [later a Royal Academician] and, 'for the 'man of ideas', in the 1930s, T. L. Poulton [an artist much used by BBC publications]. Into the mid-30s LPE introduced a lighter touch and women appeared

A 'group shot' of LPE advertisements from *Commercial Art Magazine*, 1928

Vauxhall

A high steady average – a constantly brilliant performance. At the same time the comfort, the smoothness, the security which comes of Basic Balance. As the London Distributors of this new Vauxhall 20-60 we offer you the opportunity of testing this speed – of driving yourself or being driven by us.

Let us show you the fine points of this new Vauxhall . its Basic Balance, which combines the ideals of every motorist in one great achievement ! At any time we are at your service. Call here as soon as you can, if only to enjoy testing such a car! Or send us a postcard for a fully illustrated catalogue.

All models on show. Prices from £475 — the first time any six-cylinder Vauxhall has been sold under £1000!

180 GREAT PORTLAND STREET, W.1

SHAW & KILBURN

LONDON DISTRIBUTORS FOR VAUXHALL MOTORS

Vauxhall

Planned by engineers who were also idealists – Basic Balance their ideal For Basic Balance is the proper combination of *all* the points looked for in the perfect car - speed, power, appearance, smoothness, economy ; but one of these virtues achieved at the expense of another Let us show you the new Vauxhall 20-60 - the car that has accomplished this ideal We are the London distributors of this motoring

masterpiece - that car that everyone is talking about We have these new Vauxhalls here for you to see - for you to be driven out in or to drive yourself We have the full range to show you Prices from £475! The first time any six-cylinder Vauxhall has been sold under £1,000! Call as soon as you can Or send a postcard for a complete catalogue of this epoch-making car.

180 GREAT PORTLAND STREET, W.1

SHAW & KILBURN

LONDON DISTRIBUTORS FOR VAUXHALL MOTORS

Part of a Press campaign for Shaw and Kilburn Distributors for Vauxhall Motors, 1928

' Then on, on we sped over the old canal. By gad, Troxwell, what comfort, what ease!

Flying boat, Sir, flying boat!'

B·O·A·C SPEEDBIRD ROUTES ACROSS THE WORLD
BRITISH OVERSEAS AIRWAYS CORPORATION

MOTOR HOW YOU WILL...

Mr. Mercury will give you more miles per gallon!

NATIONAL BENZOLE MIXTURE

Illustration by Peter Probyn for BOAC, 1942

Motor How You Will, National Benzole Mixture, 1951

A. V. Roe Aircraft manufacturers from *Modern Publicity*, 1930

Cadbury's Bourn-Vita's *Sleeping Beaker*, 1953

DELTA
SHOES

REX
SHOES

Showcard illustrations by Dora M Batty for Lotus , 1929

10 Minutes to Wait, Press campaign for De Reszke Minors Cigarettes, 1938

Conversation, Press campaign for the Three Nuns Tobacco, 1934

Magazine advertisement for Players No.7 cigarettes, 1953

in the visuals, albeit servilely finding men who smoked the brand more attractive or considering husbands who smoked the brand more content with their lot, making for wedded bliss! When it came to de Reske Minors, in the late 30s women [known actresses of the time], took more central roles in the advertisements, actually being shown smoking whilst having 'ten minutes to wait'.

Into the 1950s LPE were still featured as producing significant press advertising, several of its clients being the press itself – the *News Chronicle*, the *Manchester Guardian* and *The Times*, commissioning such distinguished artists as Jean Carlu, the French poster designer. A particular popular tag was the agency's 'Top people…take the Times'.

By the late 50s, like so many other of these early established agencies, LPE was being overtaken in many aspects by the Americans. George Harrison retired in 1951, and, although remaining Chairman, died in 1961. The various Sykes descendants who had joined the agency at different times, seem to have lacked the character, talents and foresight to move with the times. In 1960 LPE merged with the American agency Leo Burnett, which was to become one of the largest agencies in the world. LPE archives are held at the History of Advertising Trust.

'If you now see up and down the country,
a people better nourished, better dressed,
better in health and more attractive
in appearance, than this country
has ever shown before, credit must be
given to this unprecedented effort of
high salesmanship: to more energetic,
more thoughtful and more colourful
marketing in which complex operation
the main force is, beyond all question or
dispute, the astonishing power of bold
and persuasive advertising.'

R. J. Sykes 1936

Jean Carlu illustration for The Times, 1958

News of PRITCHARD, WOOD

Looking over other people's shoulders

PRITCHARD, WOOD & PARTNERS

Although Pritchard, Wood & Partners was a prominent advertising agency for much of the 20th century, its founders, Fleetwood Craven Pritchard and Sinclair Charles Wood, do not stand out as strongly in the history of advertising as some of the people they were to take onto their Board and employ. If Pritchard's name crops up to-day it is perhaps more frequently as his being a member of a rather eccentric family, and as the elder brother of 'Jack', the influential modernist, co-founder of Isokon [for whom Pritchard, Wood was to act as agents]. Whilst Sinclair Wood became altogether better known for his distinguished career in WWII [rising from radar operator to Assistant Director of Organisatioon at the Air Ministry], and for his sterling work on behalf of the Liberal Party.

Fleetwood Pritchard was an advertising man from the start. Educated at Pembroke College, Cambridge, and serving as Captain in the RFA in the first World War, he did his apprenticeship, as it were, initially with MacFisheries, who were, at the time, to the fore when it came to striking press advertising; and then, from 1921-2 at Crawford's agency. Wood, a grammar school boy, also served in the war, but came to advertising after a period in journalism.

Pritchard, Wood & Partners was established in 1923, at 1 Arundel Street, the Strand, subsequently moving to its modernist offices at 25 Savile Row. Later it was to use part of its offices as a 'creative centre' initially with exhibitions to keep each part of the agency au fait with what the others were doing, but later as a public exhibition space for clients to visit.

From the start the agency was research minded, Wood, in particular, being committed to market research; it could be said to be more focused on markets and consumers than design and copy, albeit it was to have some extremely well designed campaigns and make use of some distinguished artists. It appears to have served a broad range of clients with perhaps two important clusters – a technical group including Pilkington Glass, British Oxygen, Noval Alloys and Northern Aluminium; and fashion including Dent's Gloves, Saxone Shoes, Morley Stockings and, predominantly, Austin Reed.

Pritchard, Wood had been the agent for Austin Reed since the early 1920s, and was to continue to be so through to 1954, working with W. D. H. McCullogh, who was the

Left: A Light Hearted Account of Research Self advertisement for Pritchard, Wood & Partners, 1950

THERE WILL BE NO GOING BACK...

FEW things will emerge from the war in exactly the same pattern as before. Old forms are being scrapped. Others, still virile through the changing years are changing yet again. Advertising today, needs the lively mind to sense the changing trends before they come, the constructive mind to plan ahead for the new conditions that await us after the war.

There are problems to be solved. Pritchard, Wood & Partners offers the collective brains of a team of people trained to solve problems of distribution and of approach to the public mind. Those with goods or services to sell, interested in preserving and furthering their goodwill now in preparation for post war prosperity, are invited to get in touch with us.

F. C. PRITCHARD, WOOD & PARTNERS LTD
13-15 BOUVERIE STREET · LONDON · E.C.4 · CENTRAL 2080

F. C. PRITCHARD, WOOD & PARTNERS LIMITED

INCORPORATED PRACTITIONERS IN ADVERTISING

13-15 BOUVERIE STREET · LONDON · E·C·4

Telephone: Central 2080. Telegrams: Pritwoders, Fleet, London

Directors: Sinclair Wood, John Gloag, E. S. Dowdall, Gerald Butler.

Products and Services we advertise:

Aga Cookers

Allied Ironfounders Ltd. (Otto Stoves, etc.)

Aluminium Union Limited

Austin Reed Ltd.

Bayliss Jones & Bayliss Ltd.
  (Decorative Ironwork, Gates, etc.)

British Industrial Solvents Ltd.

British Resin Products Ltd.

Churchman's No. 1 Cigarettes

B. Cohen & Son Ltd. (Furniture)

Fitu & Abdo Corsets

Dormeuil Frères (Sportex Cloth)

Gyproc Products Ltd.

Halex Toothbrushes

Heal's Furniture & Fabrics

H.M. Government — Ministry of Information,
  Ministry of Home Security

Wm. Hollins & Co. Ltd.
  (Viyella Fabrics, Knitting Yarns, etc.)

Honeywill & Stein Ltd.

Izal Germicide and Toilet Rolls

Johnson & Johnson (Gt. Britain) Ltd.
  (Johnson's Baby Powder)

Luvisca Shirts and Pyjamas

Chas. Moore & Co. Ltd. (Lymm Pure Salt)

I. & R. Morley Ltd.
  (Hosiery, Underwear, Knitwear, etc.)

Old Angus Whisky

Omega Watches

Pascall's Sweets

Pilkington Brothers Limited
  (Structural and Decorative Glass)

Red, White & Blue Coffee

Red Chief Shag

Ryvita

Sandeman's Port

Saxone Shoes

Tenova Socks

Troughton & Young Ltd. (The Lighting Centre Ltd.)

Venesta Plywood & Plymax

H. Young & Co. Ltd. (Structural Steelwork)

Self advertisement, 1940

Self advertisement, 1941

Pritchard, Wood & Partners 'Remove' to Savile Row

firm's advertising manager, but who, in 1932, joined Pritchard, Wood as a copy writer, bringing the account with him. It was McCullogh who had run Austin Reed's outstanding 'New Tailoring' campaign in 1925, and who was to work with the talented Tom Purvis, who provided the illustration. Another artist who McCullough used for the firm's advertising was Fougasse, whose 'whispering men' were to feature in Austin Reed's publicity. And it was McCullough who edited and provided much of the copy for it's 'masculine' magazine, *Modern Man* which he had launched in 1929. He had an easy writing style, much as a salesman talking to a customer in a shop –

Illustration by Gordon Ransome for Austin Reed, 1952

> '*I feel that reading an advertisement is exactly the same as going into a shop; people prefer to deal with salesmen who are smiling and cheerful, but if they are impertinent, or if you feel they are laughing at you… well you just don't buy.*'

It was on the strength of his writing skills and his status within Austin Reed that Pritchard, Wood was not only to take him on, but make him a Director.

Another writer who Pritchard, Wood made a Director was John Gloag, who may possibly have met Pritchard when both worked in advertising at MacFisheries soon after WWI. Gloag had originally aspired to becoming an architect and had started studies only to be interrupted by war service. He experienced the trauma of gas poisoning and was invalided home. It was

during the war years that Gloag forewent design ambitions and turned to writing, partly combining the two on becoming technical editor of the 'Cabinet Maker'. He was, in fact, to have a distinguished career as a writer, with some twenty books to his name, largely on architecture and furnishing, these, curiously, accompanied by several successful sci-fi novels.

Gloag joined Pritchard, Wood in 1927, remaining a Director through to 1961. What his actual role was is not clear, but *Art & Industry*, in 1936, described him as 'advertising director' – a rather vague term. An off-quoted quip of Gloag's suggests that he did have direct contact with the artists being commissioned. When asked by a young designer as how much license he could have in making a drawing for a booklet cover, Gloag is reported to have replied –

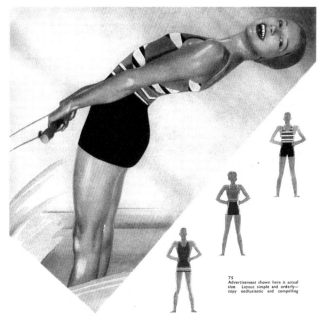

Whispering by Fougasse for Austin Reed, 1936

Bathing suits for Wolsley, magazine advertisement, 1931

Illustration by D. J. O'Connell for
Austin Reed, 1940

Illustrated Gloves for
I & R Morley Ltd, 1952

*'You can be as licentious as you like provided
you do an interesting job.'*

Whatever his exact remit Gloag certainly helped to get the name of the agency publicised, both directly, by bringing its name into the numerous articles he wrote, or indirectly, by his burgeoning reputation as a writer, a networker, and his championing of design. His continuing interest in design and its commercial application is illustrated in a rabble-rousing article appearing in *Art & Industry* in 1939 with the onset of war –

*'But for heavens sake lets get out of our heads the idea
that the creative designer is a long-haired irresponsible
sort of bloke, who is only useful in wartime when he's
doing camouflage. We should recognize that the artist
and designer are technicians of equal importance
with the engineer, and that their present and future
employment and the training of a new generation
should not be neglected if we really care seriously
for the civilization we are fighting to preserve from
spiritual and moral barbarism.'*

Although in the inter-war period Austin Reed perhaps dominated Pritchard, Wood's 'fashion' advertising, its work for other clients in the industry was considered noteworthy, certainly by the design press; Wolsey, being one example. Into the 1930s Wolsey, which had previously advertised its products under the one name, decided to give each product a brand name or feature them separately, as 'young Wolsey' or 'Wolsey Men's Underwear'. Pritchard, Wood was brought in for its press advertising and introduced some of the kind of humour it had been using for Austin Reed's. Although Wolsey was to use several agencies, Paul Jobling, in his excellent book *Man Appeal*, wrote of Pritchard Wood being 'the hallmark of Wolsey advertising between 1930 and 1932' –

> '*a clean layout, usually incorporating the company's trademark alongside an illustration of a male figure, with headlines set in Erbar bold, one of the new German sans serif typefaces…*'

And Pritchard, Wood made its mark in the advertising of technical products, which were usually only to be seen in technical journals. The agency came to the conclusion that it was infact non-technical people, particularly financial men, who played a greater part in the buying of technical products than was generally appreciated and it set out to 'sell' technical products in the general press. An example is its advertisements for British Oxygen illustrated with a Viking longboat, crafted together, implying the notion of 'welding' for which British Oxygen was noted – far-fetched but a strikingly arresting design that would have caught the reader's eye. A similar 'dissociated' image was when the agency used the humorous design duo

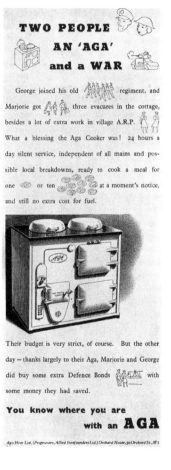

'Marjorie and George' for Aga Heat Ltd. 1941

Lewitt-Him who provided a whimsical cart-horse with copy stressing how Northern Aluminium could 'lighten the load'. A further example for that company was Pritchard, Woods' employment of the artist Anthony Dorrell who produced an image of two fish on a plate, the link being fishing trawlers having aluminium-lined holds. Other artists used by the agency for Northern Aluminium were the Australian John Bainbridge [much used by P&O], and Eric Fraser [far better known for his Radio Times' illustrations]. Much of Pritchard, Wood's 'technical' advertising seems to have taken place post-WWII when Reg Forster was its Art Director.

The agency's reputation was to be enhanced, during WWII, with its much acclaimed work for the Ministry of Transport's Road Safety campaigns. As early as 1936 the Advertising Association had written to the then Minister of Transport, Hore-Belisha, suggesting he make use of advertising for government publicity on the subject. But it was only in wartime conditions, with a mounting death toll due to the 'blackout', that the government acted on the suggestion. Pritchard, Wood & Partners was the agency chosen for an intense two-month press campaign, said to have been carried by two million newspapers. The press advertisements used shock tactics both in the headlines chosen and in illustrations. 'How many will die in the black-out tonight' was accompanied by copy continued in this tone, adding advice as to how to prevent this happening. 'World's Press News' commented on the campaign –

'We hail the new Road Safety advertising with more pleasure than usual… we hope this campaign shows the results it deserves to show; it will teach the government a thing or two about official advertising.'

Pritchard, Wood & Partners was to merge with a large American conglomerate, Interpublic Group, originally McCann Erikson. In 1968 the then managing Director, Martin Boase and some colleagues attempted what was to be a failed management buy-out. Boase, along with Gabe Massini, Stanley Pollitt and seven other directors left to form Boase, Massini, Pollitt. Pritchard, Wood was merged with other agencies within the Interpublic Group to form Wasey, Pritchard, Wood & Quadrant.

GLASS AGE PRODUCTS

Specify "Vitrolite". An opaque glass material with a hard, fire-finished surface, unaffected by water, soap or grease. It is made in black, white, ivory, pearl grey, tango, primrose, eggshell, green, turquoise, wedgwood blue, shell pink, and four agate colours: walnut, royal blue, green and golden. Also with a rolled fluted surface in most of these colours. Standard Ashlar sizes: 10" × 15", 12" × 18", 15" × 15", 14" × 21".

Issued by Pilkington Brothers Limited, St. Helens, Lancs., whose technical department is always available for consultation regarding the properties and uses of glass in architecture. Supplies can be obtained through the usual trade channels. "Vitrolite" is the registered trade mark of Pilkington Brothers Limited.

Advertisement for Pilkington Brothers Ltd, 1940

Research heralds the 3rd metal age – ALUMINIUM

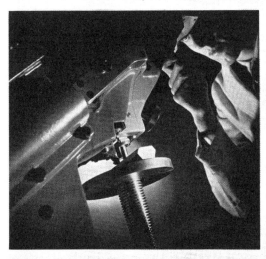

First the Bronze Age. Then the Iron Age. Now forward to the Third Metal Age: Aluminium. Because of its inexhaustible supplies of raw materials it is destined to world conquest. Because of its exceptional qualities it will influence enormously, future automobile design and manufacture. Wartime conditions may impose limitations on present supplies, but research looks ahead. As we are the largest distributors of Aluminium in the British Empire, our Research Laboratories are working unceasingly on behalf of the motor industry. Those laboratories are serving that industry.

ALUMINIUM UNION LIMITED
London • Montreal

THE ADELPHI, STRAND, LONDON, W.C.2 *and at Shanghai, Osaka, Sao Paulo, and Buenos Aires.*

Press advertisement for Aluminium Union Ltd, 1941

STUART ADVERTISING AGENCY

The Stuart Advertising Agency was set up by Hugh Stuart Menzies, who, coming from a wealthy background which would have cushioned him in such a venture, had already tested himself out, to an extent, when running Fortnum & Mason's Invalid Delicacies Department. He had also taken on responsibility for advertising and was proving frivolity and whimsy, not all that frequently found in advertising up to that time, really paid off in selling certain goods and services. Menzies light-heartedness was sufficiently balanced with ambition to make him think he could make a go independently, and, in 1922 he established his agency in Kingsway House, starting out confidently in the knowledge that he could have Fortnum & Mason as a client.

Robert Harling, who worked at the Stuart Advertising Agency for a time described Menzies as –

'...a larger-than-life figure – intelligent, funny, possessed of an unusual ability to get along with everyone from directors to bashful artists.'

Left: Edward Bawden illustrated map for Imperial Airways (details), 1934

Marcus Brumwell, who was to become his partner and eventually take over the agency, was a rather different character, with an altogether less cushioned background. Although educated at a public school, the family had insufficient funds for him to go on to university and he was to try his hand at several jobs – selling boot polish, working in motor publicity – before meeting Menzies, around 1924.

Brumwell has been described as, at core, a rather shy man, unconfident in large groups, yet like Menzies, he was a considerable networker which led him eventually to have his fingers in so many other pies.

By 1926 Brumwell had joined Menzies in Holborn, and whilst Menzies was developing the 'lighter' side of Stuart's, it was Brumwell who brought in 'modernism' to its visuals. Curiously it was through tennis that this came about, for Ben Nicholson and Henry Moore were fellow tennis players of Brumwell's wife Rene. It was through these friendships that Stuart's began to commission the likes of Graham Sutherland, John Piper, Moholy-Nagy and Paul Nash.

Brumwell expounded his attitude to the use of 'modern' art in advertising in the Penrose Annual of 1939. In this he was not writing of commercial artists, even of the outstanding ability of Tom Purvis, but of the 'non-representative' art of the time, that of his friends –

'if taken in small doses, a 'modern' design on a leaflet or a poster has, in my experience, the desired effect of awakening interest and making the eye look.'

He considered it a key aspect of an advertising agent's job to –

'look for new artists, try them out, encourage them, show them how to be practical.'

In supporting such artists Brumwell claimed that advertising agencies not only could provide them with paid work, but could educate the public's aesthetic taste, a cause he considered really mattered more than 'commercialism'. Most of the artists Stuart's used appear to have worked on a freelance basis, but the name Donald Gardner crops up with a good deal of the agency's output over the years, perhaps most frequently for the Courtauld account in the 1950s, albeit he seems to have been at Stuart's nearly as long as Brumwell himself. Gardner's name occurs as Director when the company was being sold, and he appears to have stayed on under the new ownership.

A crucial turning point for Stuart's was Menzies marrying and deciding to emigrate, around 1938-9. This not only broke the agency's ties with Fortnum & Mason, which moved its

Food is doubly precious in war time, brochure for the International Refrigeration Co, 1940

account to Colman, Prentis & Varley, an agency which was also to purloin the Shell-Mex BP account, when Jack Beddington joined them at the end of WWII.

All this necessitated Brumwell looking for investment money to keep the agency afloat and he found this with Sligh Bros. who put money in in 1939 but were bought out in 1942. Some of the shares went to Lt. Cmdr. H. C. Timewell, an employee of Stuart's who then became a member of the Board. Stuart's survived the war by working with other agencies in the Advertising Guild for government commissions. And for its own accounts Stuart's gave its advertisements a patriotic twist, as with a brochure for the International Refrigeration

Co. entitled in large script type 'Food is doubly precious in wartime'.

By 1946 Stuart's had moved west into Mayfair, to 37 Park Street, and by 1951, with Timewell no longer active, Brumwell, again riding turbulent times, became Chairman. By this time Brumwell had numerous irons in other fires, including being founder of the Institute of Contemporary Arts and of the Design Research Unit [which he referred to as 'my design company']. It is suggested that Brumwell perhaps had too many irons elsewhere, and key accounts began to be transferred. But it was Brumwell's retirement that triggered the sale of the agency to Roles & Parker in 1962.

Over its lifetime, Stuart's can be said to have been a generalist agency with clients across the industries. Of course Fortnum & Mason was key for many years and the humorous outpourings of Menzies in his 'little booklets' – 'Commentaries' with W. M. Hendy providing the whimsical illustrations and later Edward Bawden, are now collector's items. Peyton Skipworth in his Fortnum's book includes a Robert Harling quote on the relationship of Bawden and Menzies –

'His drawings were exactly attuned to Menzie's almost carefree but cunningly persuasive prose. Few commercial partnerships between writer and artist have been more rewarding.'

Another impressive Stuart's account was that for Imperial Airways, a result of a merger of early air transport companies in 1924. It was a heady time, at the start of the British Aviation industry; faced with competition from abroad, advertising became of key importance. Initially Imperial Airways had turned to Charles Higham and seemed reasonably content until Bill Snowden Gamble was appointed publicity manager for the Airways in 1931. Brumwell recorded Stuart's taking over from Higham's –

'...we studied their advertising and asserted that we could double their turnover without increasing their appropriation. This we succeeded in doing, and in four months.'

Brumwell was to draw on a number of his friends as well as up and coming young designers to produce striking modernist designs including Ben Nicholson, John Piper, Edward Bawden, James Gardner and Frank Newbould. Brumwell's son, Joe, wrote of this work –

'With this combination of strong design and first class production [much printed at the Curwen Press], the overall visual identity of Imperial reflected the excitement of air travel as well as a competent and caring operator with the highest standard of safety, comfort and efficiency.'

Illustration by Richard Taylor for Fortnum and Mason, 1939

Illustration by Edward Bawden for Fortnum and Mason, 1939

E. McKnight Kauffer invitation to Fortnum and Mason's
new season's fashion, 1933

Cover of leaflet for Imperial Airways, Illustration by
John Piper, 1939

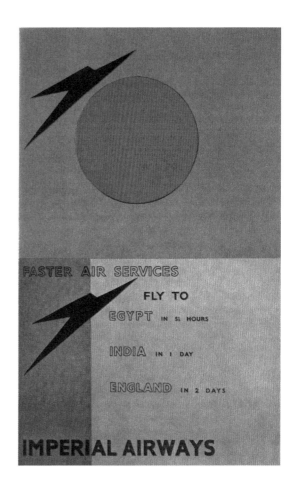

Posters and leaflets designed by Ben Nicholson for
Imperial Airways, 1939

IMPERIAL AIRWAYS

James Gardiner illustration for the new Imperial Airways routes, 1938

Booklet for Imperial Airways designed by Lee Elliot, 1935

Booklet for Imperial Airways designed by Moholy-Nagy, 1939

Press advertisement for Imperial Airways, 1939

Hans Erni illustration for Imperial Airways, 1939

Edward Bawden illustration for Imperial Airways, 1938

The artists that contributed most, and caused the greatest stir, was Theyre Lee-Elliott, now largely forgotten and certainly under-rated when his name does crop up. He was something of a polymath – a sportsman who read theology at Cambridge, [played table tennis for England], a good commercial artist [trained at Central and the Slade], and a 'fine artist' of religious subjects [combining his talent and his interest towards the end of his career]. Lee-Elliott did a range of designs for Imperial Airways – for posters, booklets, and so on, but is best known for creating the Airway's symbol 'Speedbird'. In this it is said he was influenced by McKnight Kauffer's symbolic birds produced for a Daily Herald poster in 1918. Lee-Elliott described using just a few diagonal lines to represent speed and a 'nick' to give the impression of birds in flight. Speedbird appeared on most everything to do with the company apart from its planes, even on fabric designed by Betty Joel, a major furniture and interior designer of the 1920s and 30s.

And a third client, with which Stuart's will forever be associated was Shell-Mex BP. Jack Beddington, Shell's publicity manager, had long been a fan of Stuart's, since his father had sent him the 'Commentaries' when he was working out in the Far East. Stuart's were to carry the Shell account until its own advertising subsidiary, Regent Advertising Service, was established in the 1930s.

Stuart's early campaigns for Shell focused on the 'pull' of the product with such images as fish caught on line, men pulling leavers, and so on. But Stuart's very soon turned to the notion

E. McKnight Kauffer illustration for Shell, *1930*

John Reynolds illustration for Shell, 1931

John Reynolds illustration for Shell, 1931

John Reynolds illustration for Shell, 1929

Rex Whistler illustration for Shell, 1931

of 'speed' with onlookers getting a glimpse of cars flashing by, obviously run on Shell petrol, with the tag 'That's Shell that is' soon to be changed to 'That's Shell that was'. And it was the artist John Reynolds who was to develop the iconic images that were to accompany the new tag. *Commercial Art* in 1931 could hardly contain its excitement –

> *'The advertising manager of Shell, Mr. J. L. Beddington, whose enthusiasm and discernment have contributed to this striking result, is to be congratulated on the bold course that has been taken.'*

The 'bold course' was to advertise something technical using humour. When the Regent Advertising Service took over it built on Stuart's success using Bawden for its series punning on British place names, but turning to Hans Schleger for a 'modernist' touch.

At a dinner in his honour in 1964, Brumwell spoke of what Stuart's meant to him personally –

> *'Stuart's has been an exceptional group... I have tried to treat everyone alike as human beings, members of our team, all reasonably equal [some more equal than others], plenty of open communication... I think the result was a jolly nice unstrained group with a very high standard of work and sincerity, resulting in a rather special reputation.'*

E. Mcknight Kauffer illustation for Shell, 1932

89

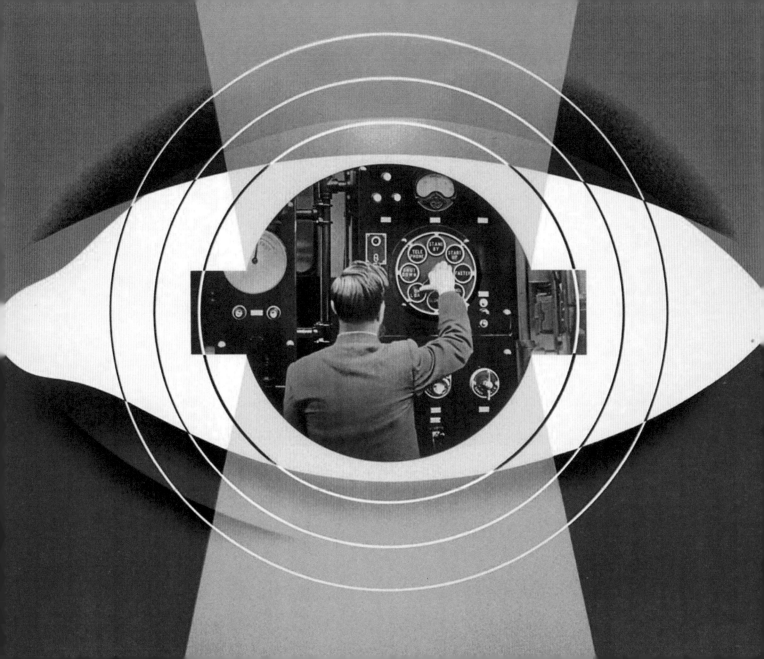

C. VERNON & SONS LTD.

There might be an argument against including Vernon as one of the more important advertising agencies of the inter-war years, for little is recorded of Vernon himself or of the development and demise of his agency, and, over the years, they appear to have handled relatively few major accounts. But although Vernon was not a self-publicist, Percy Bradshaw, a leading commentator on advertising in the 1920s, credited him as being one of the industry's outstanding figures, to be rated up there with the Higham's and the Crawford's. And Vernon's agency was rare, in one respect, in that it had, associated with it, for some fifty years, one artist – James Fitton – much as Crawford's had Ashley. Indeed, at one time Crawford tried to filch Fitton from Vernon. Fitton not only became the agency's Art Director and a direct influence on the growth of Vernon's, but, parallel to his career in advertising, achieved the status of a Royal Academician; no other advertising artist over this period so successfully had a foot in both camps, as it were.

Very little is known of Vernon's upbringing or early career but by the turn of the century he had set himself up in his own advertising agency initially in Newgate Street, to the north of St. Pauls. By the 1920s he had relocated to Holborn Viaduct, and, later, moved westwards to Stratford Place, a cul-de-sac near Bond Street underground station. Vernon, a Londoner, also had a northern branch in Liverpool, largely dealing with smallish firms in the region but possibly having some connection with the agency's work for Cunard.

Vernon was someone who liked to work quietly in the background. Yet in his time he was to hold important positions in the advertising world as Chairman of District N14 [Britain] of the Associated Advertising Clubs of the World and Vice-President of the Advertising Association. In relation to his style of operating his own agency he impresses as a sympathetic boss and a respecter of the commercial use of talent. He was to argue for both copywriters and artists having their work signed and generally championed their roles –

'I believe the future of the Advertising profession is full of promise, provided that Advertising Agents allow, and are permitted to allow, their copy writers and commercial artists to develop their allowed arts to the full.'

Left: *Behind the Seen*, James Fitton for London Transport, 1948

James Fitton poster design for London Transport, 1948

WEAR OR CARRY
SOMETHING WHITE

James Fitton design for London Transport, 1941

He poured scorn on those agencies that merely took 'images' from 'fine' artists or the words of 'literary' writers, for he saw as valid specialisms the roles of copy writer and commercial artist.

'I know of no great novelist who is also a first class copy writer, and, with apologies to L.M.S. I know of no Royal Academician who is also a first class commercial artist.'

Of course he was mistaken in this, for his own Art Director, who became one of the leading commercial artists of his time, was also to achieve the accolade of being appointed a Royal Academician. But James Fitton was to run the two strands of his career parallel, and what Vernon was complaining about was the mere use of a piece of 'fine' art plus typography as an advertisement, or similarly a piece of literature with a loosely related image above it. He saw commercial art as a whole package, a total design to include image, typography and lay-out. Yet it was some of Fitton's 'fine' art work, on show at the Leicester Galleries in the 1920s, that led Frank Pick of London Transport to realize the attractiveness of Fitton for some of his publicity posters.

Not without an aesthetic sensibility himself, [his office is said to have been adorned with a Holbein print above the fireplace and an American poster on the opposite wall], Vernon seems to have both venerated his artists as well as challenged them –

Trademark designed by James Fitton for
C. Vernon & Sons, 1928

*'The commercial artist is a creative artist –
a thinker and a planner, a learner and a watcher,
an observer and a traveller. He never ceases to
study, and always strives for originality; above all
else he is a designer.'*

And James Fitton appears to have come up to Vernon's expectations. Fitton had come from a politically active, working class family in Lancashire. His schooling was sporadic due to a bungled ear operation that left him partially deaf. On leaving school he tried his hand at textile designing and on a newspaper in districts near his home in Oldham, at the same time attending evening classes with Adolfe Valette at the Manchester School of Art. Coming down to London [around 1919/20] he worked at a printers, continuing his art education at the Central School of Arts and Crafts.

It was around 1928 that he joined Vernon's and from when his work was first noted in the commercial art press, some in a style 'Commercial Art' referred to as 'modernist non-realistic', including as an example a label Fitton did for the agency itself, one that became its trademark. That Fitton committed himself to commercial art as a career and stayed content with being at the one agency all his working life, may partly have been due to family responsibilities, partly due to his finding free-lancing onerous, as well as to his finding his talents well-suited to the work and the work, in turn, giving satisfaction.

Fitton's name featured frequently in the design press attached to the advertising for a wide range of clients including Boots Pharmacy, Lagonda cars, Mullard Wireless, Colman's Mustard, and Parker Knoll furniture. And all of this running parallel to his work as a 'fine' artist and to a good deal of satirical cartooning for magazines. He had joined a thriving agency and helped build it further.

Fitton, a good-humoured raconteur, who his fellow art student at Manchester, one L. S. Lowry described as 'the nicest person I knew', developed close friendships with many of his clients, which no doubt helped the agency keep accounts, although that was not what motivated him. *Art & Industry* commending his considerable output for Vernon's over the years wrote of him in 1937 –

> '*To advertising design he contributes a talent for bright and sometimes strident colour, a gift of humorous draughtsmanship, leaning towards caricature, an ability to make his designs tell.*'

One of Vernon's most noted campaigns was for the Post Office Telephone Service in 1932 –

> '*The Post Office Advertising Campaign for the telephone has contributed to a net increase of 72,000 telephone stations – the largest recorded increase in telephones of any country.*'

Part of the Post Office advertising campaign for the Telephone, 1932

The Carriage Awaits, James Fitton

A Bolt to the Blue, James Fitton

James Fitton design for Russian Oil Products

Poster Stamps by James Fitton for E and G Berry Ltd, 1928

James Fitton Booklet cover (left) and Showcard (right) for Frederick Theak & Co, 1928

James Fitton design for Lagonda, 1931

Press advertisement for Warner Fabrics, 1940

SULTANAS

are

CHEAP AND PLENTIFUL

Huge quantities of delicious sultanas are now in the shops—they are even more plentiful than pre-war. You can buy them at a remarkably low price—even *less* than pre-war. Sultanas give you extra natural sugar for many excellent dishes, cakes, pastries and puddings, and they save your sugar ration.

FROM 6d. lb.

ACCORDING TO QUALITY

for more energy

Sultana campaign for the Ministry of
Food, 1941

Sir Kingsley Wood, Postmaster-General

It was estimated that the Post Office increased its revenue by a million pounds a year by the campaign. The advertisements carried quite large blocks of copy, but these were lightened by images of telephones and their users. Initially the telephone itself took pride of place, but early advertisements were followed by examples of users – telling grandma that she had a new grandson, daddy talking to his little girl, general gossiping, and so on. Finally the campaign advertisements became self-congratulatory – '1,600,000,000 calls a year'. *Commercial Art* wrote of the campaign –

> '*In every advertisement, whether the theme is usefulness, emergency or complicated information, the miracle of the telephone service is conveyed in simple terms and brought within the easy understanding of the man in the street and the housewife in the home… The whole of the press advertising for the Post Office Telephone Service during 1932 was created and produced by C. Vernon & Sons Ltd. and they are entitled to congratulate themselves on a really great achievement.*'

Fitton's name was not associated with this campaign, possibly because if its use of photography, whereas he featured largely in Vernon's wartime campaigns, particularly those run by the Ministry of Food. The majority of the government's wartime

Milk - The essential food for growing children,
James Fitton for the Ministry of Food 1941

A clear plate means a clear conscience,
James Fitton for the Ministry of Food, 1940

Turn over a new leaf,
James Fitton for the Ministry of Food, 1943

publicity was channelled through the Ministry of Information, one exception being those concerned with food. Vernons was involved in these, some of its contributions made just by the agency, some in collaboration with other agencies. Rationing was introduced in January 1940 to ensure everyone got a basic diet, and the government, anxious that the scheme should be run successfully, approached the Advertising Association, which recommended Vernons along with other agencies. Vernon's first advertisements appeared in all the national dailies and major provincial newspapers by November, of first importance 'Your New Ration Book, how to register with the shops'.

The Ministry of Food took a number of approaches to the challenge of limited supplies – eat more of what was available, what more could be produced at home, cook more efficiently, reduce waste etc. Vernons were used for hyping the consumption of dry fruits, running the campaign along the lines 'Sultanas are Cheap and Plentiful'; and with other agencies for prevent waste campaigns – 'Food is the munition of war, Don't waste it'. Fitton's best remembered contributions were colourful posters such as 'Turn over a new leaf, eat vegetables to enjoy good health', 'A clear plate means a clear conscience'; and one encouraging children to drink milk 'The Backbone of Young Britain'. Other wartime work by Vernons was for London Transport warning of problems incurred by the blackout. Fitton had already done some entertainment posters for London Transport relating to his interest in popular entertainment, and he was to team up with its Publicity Officer, Harold Hutchinson to do a light-hearted book on babies – *The first six months are the worst.*

Vernon & Sons were in their halcyon days from the 1920s through to the 1940s. Other members of the Vernon family had joined the agency at various times; a Charles Vernon and a Percy H. Vernon are mentioned occasionally, but little is known of their length of stay or their roles. Vernon, himself, died in 1965 and although the agency ran on for a time, unlike other agencies it appears to have been dissolved rather than merged.

The backbone of young Britain,
James Fitton for the Ministry of Food, 1942

EPILOGUE

World War II can be seen to have been a watershed between the two 'golden' ages of advertising. Advertising didn't cease between the wars but was severely restricted not only by the scarcity of supplies of paper and print but also by the limited consumer commodities around to be advertised, with much of manufacturing given up to munitions and the importing of goods difficult.

What had happened to advertising in the decades following WWI to justify the attribute 'golden'. Well firstly a new profession came into being. Advertisements were no longer cobbled together in printers' workshops by hacks but were the productions of a new breed of specialists – copywriters, commercial artists [to morph into graphic designers], accounts executives. And these were supported and promoted in their activities by burgeoning advertising clubs, professional bodies and advertising industry's related newspapers and journals.

And those caught up in this first wave seem not to have been content with merely following a brief, doing as good a job as possible in helping to sell goods and services, but began to see their work as having missionary status – raising the standard of British art and consumer taste; changing the way organisations operated; even influencing the way governments functioned. They saw themselves as educator, persuaders, change agents – and that is what many of them became.

These early advertising agencies grew through the energies, talents and ambitions of some exceptional individuals; and they tended to thrive and wane as the lives of these key figures blossomed and faded. Many of these agencies faltered and lost momentum on the retirement and/or death of their founders, born in Victorian times and leaving the scene, one way or another, in the 1940s and 50s. Myriads of small and medium-sized agencies either folded or were engulfed in the mergers and amalgamations of the post-war years.

As if to pronounce the death of the old and the birth of the new, advertising shifted its base from its original roots around Fleet St, Kingsway and the Strand to Soho and Fitzrovia – the taverns and restaurants of Charlotte Street replacing those of Covent Garden.

The incredible optimism that, against reality, permeated the austerity years following WWII, the rebuilding of Britain in every sense and sphere, brought in a second golden age to British advertising – more complex technically, more subtle and indirect in its messaging – sophistication was in, whimsy and sentimentality now history, photography and film ousting hand drawn. The first golden age of British advertising was not only gone, but largely forgotten.

'In advertising the artist is everything.
For, in commerce as in life, his function is to
improve reality — to make everyday objects
arresting, interesting and glamorous.'

- Saxon Mills

Penrose Annual, 1933

Other books by Ruth Artmonsky

Jack Beddington, a footnote man, 2006
The School Prints, 2006
Art for Everyone, 2007
A Snapper up of Unconsidered Trifles, 2008
Bringers of Good Tidings, 2009
Shipboard Style, 2010
'Do you want it good or do you want it Tuesday?', 2011
Designing Women, 2012
The Pleasures of Printing, 2013
Showing Off, 2013
Exhibiting Ourselves, 2014
Moving the Hearts and Minds of Men, 2014
Unashamed Artists, 2014
Art for the Ear, 2015

Here's to Your Health, (with Stella Harpley), 2015
Tom Purvis: Art for the Sake of Money, 2015
The Best Advertising Course in Town, 2015
Powering the Home, 2016
From Palaces to Pre-Fabs, 2017

P&O, a history, Shire Publications, 2012
P&O, across the oceans, across the years, Antique Collectors' Club, 2012

The Design series published by the Antique Collectors' Club –
Design, Lewitt-Him, 2008
Design, FHK Henrion, 2011
Design, Enid Marx, 2013

Left: Edward Bawden Illustrates a map for Imperial Airways, Stuart Advertising, 1934